Alpha Youth Film Series Discussion Guide

Published in North America by Alpha North America, 1635 Emerson Lane, Naperville, IL 60540

© 2014 Alpha International, Holy Trinity Brompton, Brompton Road, London SW7 1JA, UK

Alpha Youth Film Series Discussion Guide

All rights reserved. No part of this guide or any other Alpha publication may be reproduced or transmitted in any form or by any means, electronic or mechanical, including photocopy, recording or any information storage and retrieval system, without permission in writing from the copyright holder or the expressly authorized agent thereof. Where an Alpha publication is offered free of charge the fee is waived on condition the publication is used to run or promote Alpha and should not be subject to any subsequent fee or charge. This resource may not be modified or used for any commercial purpose without permission in writing from the copyright holder or the expressly authorized agent thereof.

This edition first printed by Alpha North America in 2014

Printed in the United States of America

Scripture in this publication is from the Holy Bible, New International Version (NIV), Copyright 1973, 1978, 1984 International Bible Society, used by permission of Zondervan. All rights reserved.

New Living Translation (NLT). Holy Bible. New Living Translation copyright © 1996, 2004, 2007 by Tyndale House Foundation. Used by permission of Tyndale House Publishers Inc., Carol Stream, Illinois 60188. All rights reserved.

English Standard Version (ESV). The Holy Bible, English Standard Version Copyright © 2001 by Crossway Bibles, a division of Good News Publishers.

New American Standard Bible (NASB). Copyright © 1960, 1962, 1963, 1968, 1971, 1972, 1973, 1975, 1977, 1995 by The Lockman Foundation

Holman Christian Standard Bible (HCSB). Copyright © 1999, 2000, 2002, 2003, 2009 by Holman Bible Publishers, Nashville Tennessee. All rights reserved.

ISBN 978-1-938328-60-2

Table of Contents

Introduction	4
How to Use	5
Life: Is This It?	8
Jesus: Who Is Jesus?	12
Cross: Why Did Jesus Die?	18
Faith: How Can I Have Faith?	23
Prayer: Why and How Do I Pray?	28
Bible: Why and How Do I Read the Bible?	33
Follow: How Does God Guide Us Into Full Life?	38
Spirit: Who Is the Holy Spirit and What Does He Do?	43
Fill: How Can I Be Filled With the Holy Spirit?	49
Evil: How Can I Resist Evil?	54
Healing: Does God Heal Today?	60
Church: What About the Church and Telling Others?	65
End Notes	70

Discussion Guide

A Note from Ben and Jason

Dear Small Group Host,

Here is the secret about the Alpha Youth Film Series: small groups are the most important part. We spent thousands of hours making this series, but it's just a spark. The impact of Alpha is only possible because of people like you; small group leaders who take the spark and lead a conversation where youth feel heard, respected, and loved. That's what students will remember and that's what will impact their lives. We need you more than you need these videos. We are praying for you as you encounter bizarre questions, awkward silences and stunning stories. You are going to do great. Keep one ear to the guests and the other to Jesus. It's not the words that you share, but the way you listen, that will make the difference.

Much love,

Ben + Jason
Hosts of the Alpha Youth Film Series

How To Use

It's Just A Guide
+ This Discussion Guide is a tool that can help every Alpha small group host. Each chapter follows the outline of the corresponding episode. It highlights the important points, helps you remember the key quotes and verses, and provides you with loads of intriguing discussion questions to keep things lively. Use it to get an idea of where the episode is going and what's been covered. It's designed to help you, not limit you. The conversation in your small group is not limited to the questions written in this book or the points we've highlighted. It's all here as a springboard to help you take the conversation further.

Not A Secret
+ Don't feel like you need to keep the content of this guide a secret from the guests at your table. We wrote it knowing that someone in your small group will want to steal it from you to see what's in here. Guests will be excited to know that you have some of the quotes and verses handy so you can come back to them in conversation.

Three Questions
+ Each episode is designed to be **paused three times** for group discussion (prompted by on-screen questions and street interviews). A countdown signals the end of each discussion break. The street interviews are meant to spark ideas and opinions and help create conversation. We've highlighted these questions in the discussion guide so you know what's coming and where you are at in the session.

Supporting Questions
+ Sometimes the question on the screen doesn't spark enough conversation so we have included several supporting questions to help you keep the conversation alive and capture the imagination of guests. Don't feel limited to these. You can be creative and throw some other questions into the mix.

Main Points
+ We have gone through each episode and highlighted the main points for you. This will help you navigate where we are going and where we have been. It will also help you facilitate conversation and remind the group of what has been said.

Verses & Quotes
+ We put some of the most important and interesting quotes from each episode in here. These seem to come up in conversation quite often. Instead of saying, "You know when Jason and Ben said something like…" you will know exactly what was said. We included Bible verses with references so you can come back to them in conversation and point to where it is in the Bible.

More Questions
+ The three breaks for conversation throughout each episode are just the beginning. We have included a handful of follow-up questions to help you lead a time of discussion after each episode is done. We recommend 10-20 minutes. Don't feel like you need to follow these questions exactly. Choose a few, mix up the order, and add your own to the mix. Let the conversation grow naturally as the guests respond with their own questions from the episode.

Register Online with Alpha Builder
(alphausa.org/run or run.alphacanada.org)

+ By registering online, you will be given free access to a suite of support materials to help you plan, promote, and run Alpha. Resources include:

- Digital discussion guide
- Customizable promo materials
- Sample session schedules
- Trailers
- Team roles
- Feedback forms

Top Tips For Great Small Group Hosts

+ Watch the training videos (Seriously. They are crucial to running a successful Alpha and will help you a lot. You will think: "Man, I'm sure glad I watched these training videos").

+ Remember names.

+ Pray (this will also help you remember everyone's name).

+ Be 100% committed.

+ Show up early, leave late.

+ Keep the conversation alive.

+ Be positive.

+ End the small group on time.

4 Rules For Every Small Group

+ You don't have to talk if you don't want to.

+ You can ask or say just about anything.

+ Respect each other by listening to and allowing different opinions.

+ Keep things confidential when you leave the group.

....

What Is Alpha?

Alpha is a series of interactive sessions that freely explore the basics of the Christian faith. More than 30 million people have experienced Alpha in 169 countries and in 112 different languages. Alpha runs in church buildings, restaurants, coffee shops and homes all around the globe. Typically Alpha is done over 10 weeks and includes food, a short talk and a discussion at the end where you can share your thoughts. Alpha really is for anyone who's curious. The talks are designed to encourage conversation and explore the basics of the Christian faith in a friendly, honest and informal environment.

> **Life with Jesus is like seeing clearly for the first time.**

Episode ONE | Life

Life

Many of us have asked the big questions: What is life all about? Is there a God? Why am I here? Alpha is an invitation to spend some time exploring these big questions by looking at the life and words of Jesus.

Question One

If you only had 24 hours left to live, what would you do?

Imagine money is limitless and travel is instant.
As each person answers this question, ask them to introduce themselves.

- Who would you spend your last day with?
- What's something you have always wanted to do? (e.g. Bucket List)
- If you could travel anywhere in the world for vacation, where would it be? Why?

Alpha is all about asking honest questions about faith, life and God.

Question Two

Why do you think people find it awkward to talk about their religious beliefs?

- Do you think there is an unspoken social rule that says, "Keep religion and spiritual thoughts to yourself"?
- Do you ever talk about religion or God with your friends?
- Why do some people think talking about religion is offensive? Is there a way to talk about it without being offensive?

"Jesus answered, 'I am the way and the truth and the life.'"
- John 14:6

I Am The Way

+ "You can have everything in the world and still be the loneliest man."[1]
- *Freddie Mercury, former lead singer of Queen*

+ Jesus claims to be the way to a loving and lasting relationship with God.

I Am The Truth

+ "When we're talking about facts, if something is true, isn't it true for everyone? And if something is not true, isn't it **not** true for anyone?" - *Jason*

+ "Christianity is a statement which, if false, is of no importance, and if true, of infinite importance. The one thing it cannot be is moderately important."[2]
- *C.S. Lewis, author of The Chronicles of Narnia*

+ In Jesus, we discover that truth isn't just a set of ideas but a person you can know.

I Am The Life

+ It's possible to be alive but not truly living.

+ "So many things creep into our lives and take away from the life God designed for us: fear, insecurity, addictions, guilt, hopelessness." - *Jason*

+ "I realized the hunger in my heart was still there. I had everything I thought I needed, but there was still something missing. There was a longing in my heart for something truer and deeper – it was a longing for life." - *Ben*

Question Three

Assuming God is real, if you could ask Him one question, what would you ask?

As people answer this question, write down the answers so you can look back at them in later weeks.

....

If you live to be 70 years old, you will spend:

+ 20 years and 3 months asleep
+ 10 years and 5 months watching TV
+ 7 years and 6 months eating and drinking
+ 5 years and 9 months in some form of transport
+ 18 months waiting in line
+ 6 months at red lights

....

"You have approximately 570,000 hours left to live and we want to invite you to spend less than 24 of them with us on Alpha."
 — *Jason*

....

More Questions (choose a few)

- How did you end up at Alpha?
- What are you hoping to learn about?
- Do you have any questions about life that you're hoping to get answered?
- What did you think about today's episode?
- What stood out to you?

> He came into the mess of this world and revealed Himself to you and to me.

Episode TWO | Jesus

Discussion Guide

Jesus

Jesus is the most well-known man to ever walk the Earth. The Gospels describe Jesus teaching thousands about the kingdom of God, performing miracles all over Israel, being crucified, and rising from the dead. Christians believe that Jesus is God and that everyone is invited to have a relationship with Him.

Question One

Have you ever had an encounter with a celebrity?

It's a good idea to have everyone introduce themselves again.

- If you could meet anyone—dead or alive, in all of history—who would you like to meet?

....

Who Is Jesus?

+ "There are no reliable historians or anthropologists who would deny that He lived." - *Ben*

+ Jesus' life marks the dividing point between the two main eras of history, BCE and CE (until recently, BC and AD). *See image on page 14.*

+ Jesus has made a bigger impact upon the world than anyone.

+ Thousands of people would gather together to hear Jesus speak, and many came to Him to be healed of sickness and disease.

+ Christians believe Jesus was not just a good man, but that He **was** and **is** God.

+ *"Christ is the visible image of the invisible God."* - *Colossians 1:15*

+ "Christ says, 'I am God Incarnate.' So what you're left with is either Christ was who He said He was, or a complete nutcase. I'm not joking here. The idea that the entire course of civilization for over half the globe could have its fate changed and turned upside-down by a nutcase – for me, that's far-fetched."[3] - *Bono (U2)*

Question Two
Why do you think Jesus is so famous?

- Why do you think a man from Israel who lived 2000 years ago is still talked about today?
- Growing up, did you hear much about Jesus?
- What sorts of things did you hear?

....

What Did Jesus Do?

+ The Gospels are eyewitness accounts of the life of Jesus.

  + Because of Textual Criticism, we can be sure that we have an accurate version of the original Gospel texts. *See image on page 14*
  + "He taught things we still live by today: *'Do to others as you would have them do to you; turn the other cheek; and forgive those who do you wrong.'*" - *Ben*

  + He healed the sick and performed miracles.

  + He claimed to be God. "Jesus said to His followers: *'If you've seen me, you've seen the Father.'* And then another time He said: *'I and the Father are one.'*" - *Ben*

  + In the 33 years of His life, He fulfilled over 300 prophecies, 29 of them on the day He died.

+ The Gospels explain that Jesus rose from the grave and appeared to His disciples and many others.

+ C.S. Lewis says this: *"We're faced then, with a frightening alternative. Either the man we're talking about was and is just who He said or else insane, or worse. Now, it seems to me obvious that He was neither a lunatic nor a fiend: and consequently, however strange or terrifying or unlikely it may seem, I have to accept the view that He was and is God."*[4]

Question Three

What parts of the life of Jesus stand out to you?

- Is there any specific story or message about Jesus that stands out to you? Why? *(Examples from the episode: He healed a man with leprosy; He healed a crippled man and forgave his sins; thousands gathered to hear Him teach; He was killed on a cross; and He appeared to His friend Thomas after He came back to life from the dead.)*
- What, if anything, about Jesus' life do you find hard to believe? Why?
- What do you think about His claim to be God?

....

Doubt And Faith

+ It's natural to doubt the claims and resurrection of Jesus. His disciple Thomas had a hard time believing until he saw Jesus alive again.

+ "It's by looking at the life, death and resurrection of Jesus that we discover evidence for God's existence." - *Jason*

+ *"Because you have seen me, you have believed; Blessed are those who have not seen and yet have believed."* - John 20:29

More Questions (choose a few)

- What did you think about today's episode?
- What stood out to you?
- Why do you think the life of one man has had such an impact on the world? (Whether you believe He was God or not.)
- What do you think about Jesus fulfilling hundreds of prophecies written hundreds of years before He was born? (Prophecies about where He was born, how He was betrayed, how He died, etc.)
- Can you imagine how Thomas must have felt when he saw Jesus standing in front of him after Jesus had come back from the dead?
- What do you think about the Christian claim that Jesus came back to life after three days?

Discussion Guide

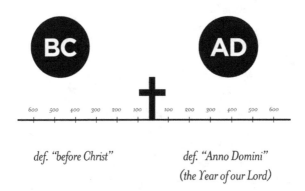

def. "before Christ"

def. "Anno Domini"
(the Year of our Lord)

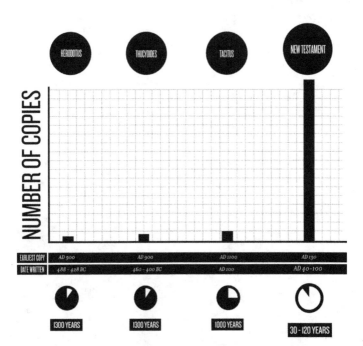

> **God cleared the path so that we can be close to Him.**

Episode THREE | Cross

Cross

In this session, we want to answer the question, "Why does Jesus' death on a cross matter to us today?" Jesus' death and resurrection break the power of sin in our lives and make it possible for us to have a relationship with God. Jesus' death is God's love on display for all of us.

Question One

What is one of your most physically painful experiences?

- Have you ever crashed a bicycle or fallen off a skateboard or a trampoline or something similar?
- Do you have any cool scars?

....

What Is The Cross?

+ Crucifixion was an ancient form of execution used by the Romans.

+ "Famous people are usually remembered for the great events of their life, but Jesus, the most famous person in history, seems to be equally remembered for His death on a cross." - *Ben*

+ "For *God so loved the world that he gave his one and only Son, that whoever believes in him will not perish but have eternal life.*" - *John 3:16*

+ "*I live by faith in the Son of God, who loved me and gave himself for me.*" - *Galatians 2:20*

+ Just as Maximilian Kolbe died to give another man life, Jesus died to give us life.

Question Two

How would you define sin? And do you see it in the world around you?

- Do you think the problems of the world are getting worse or better?
- Jason and Ben said, "Sin is not just in the world around us but also in each one of us." How do you feel about this idea?
- Who should decide what is right and what is wrong?

....

What Is Sin?

+ God doesn't compare us to one another to see if we are good people or not.

+ *"For everyone has sinned; we all fall short of God's glorious standard."* - *Romans 3:23*

Sin Has A Polluting Effect
+ "It's not about the amount of sin, a lot or a little; sin and selfishness have polluted our entire heart." - *Ben*

+ The bad things that we do are evidence that we're broken.

Sin Has An Addictive Power
+ We find ourselves being tempted to do things we know are wrong, and worse, we find ourselves doing the very things we didn't want to do.

+ *"I don't understand my own actions, I do not do what I want and I do the very thing I hate."* - *Romans 7:15 (paraphrased)*

Sin Has A Cost
+ "The Bible says that there's a cost, and that what we earn from our sinfulness is a spiritual death." - *Ben*

Sin Destroys Relationships

+ "This is the most tragic result of sin: it destroys our relationship with God." - *Jason*

+ A lie can wreck a friendship; cheating can break a family; and, in much the same way, sin breaks our relationship with God.

Jesus Died To Free Us From Sin

The Judge And His Friend

+ "Even though the debt is too big and the wall is too high, God provided a solution." - *Jason*

+ His death was the payment for our debt of sin.

Sacrificial Lamb

+ When Jesus died on the cross, He took our guilt and sin on Himself so that we could be forgiven and free.

+ In ancient Jewish culture, it was normal to deal with the guilt of sin by sacrificing animals like sheep and goats. The death of an animal represented payment for the people's sin. Jesus put an end to this system by becoming the final sacrifice for the sins of mankind.

+ *"Each of us has turned to our own way; and the Lord has laid on him the iniquity of us all." - Isaiah 53:6*

Question Three

Do you think there is a difference between the death of Jesus and other religious leaders, martyrs or war heroes?

- Why or why not?
- Does the death of Jesus have any personal meaning to you?

Jesus Died to Free Us From Sin (continued)

+ God Himself carried the weight of our sin to bring us into a relationship with Him.

+ *"In Christ, God was reconciling the world to Himself."*
- 2 Corinthians 5:19

+ *"But he was pierced for our transgressions, he was crushed for our iniquities; the punishment that brought us peace was on him, and by his wounds we are healed." - Isaiah 53:5*

+ Jesus' resurrection proves that He has authority over sin and death.

A Son Welcomed Home
+ "You can be forgiven of all the wrong you've done and be given a fresh start." - *Jason*

+ Because of the cross, we can have a relationship with our heavenly Father.

More Questions (choose a few)

- How did you feel about today's episode?
- What stood out to you?
- Do you think it's fair to say that everyone has sinned?
- When Jason and Ben showed the "good person test", they said that God doesn't compare us to one another to determine if we are good or not ("God doesn't share our rating system."). What do you think about that idea?
- In this episode there were a few different pictures used to describe what Jesus did on the cross: a father welcoming his son home, a judge paying for his friend's crime, and a priest killing a lamb as a sacrifice. Which of these pictures stood out to you the most? Why?

> **A relationship with God is for anyone. It's unconditional. And it's everlasting.**

Episode FOUR | Faith

Faith

Christianity is not a club someone joins. It's the gift of a life-changing relationship with Jesus. It requires faith—not a blind leap—but a step of faith based on the truth about who Jesus is and what He has done.

Question One

What is one of the scariest things you've ever done?

- If given the chance, what extreme sport would you want to try?

What Does It Mean To Be A Christian?

+ "Going to church doesn't make you a Christian any more than hanging out at McDonalds makes you a Big Mac." - *Ben*

+ Becoming a Christian is beginning a life-changing relationship with God through Jesus. It is a unique experience for everyone.

+ We can have confidence in our relationship with God because it stands firmly on the promises of God the Father, on the life, death and resurrection of Jesus, and on the assurance that comes from the Holy Spirit.

What Is A Friendship With God Like?

Everyone Is Invited To Have A Friendship With God

+ *"Here I am! I stand at the door and knock. If anyone hears my voice and opens the door, I will come in and eat with that person, and they with me."* - *Revelation 3:20*

+ No matter who you are or what you have done, you are invited to have friendship with God.

+ "Jesus spent time with prostitutes, cheaters and sinners. They felt loved and accepted by Him." - *Jason*

Friendship With God Is Unconditional

+ Friendships with people can be fickle and conditional, but a relationship with God is different. It's not based on how we feel from one day to the next; it's rooted in the unchanging promises of God that are found in the Bible.

+ *"Never will I leave you; and never will I forsake you."* - Hebrews 13:5

+ "I've made a ton of wrong choices in my life, but God has never left me, and I know He never will." - *Jason*

Friendship With God Is Everlasting

+ *"For God so loved the world that he gave his one and only Son, that whoever believes in him shall not perish but have eternal life."* - John 3:16

Question Two

How can God love people no matter what they have done?

- Why is it hard for some people to believe that God loves them?
- What do you think about the claim that God forgives and loves us despite the wrong that we have done?

....

What Is Grace?

+ *"For it is by grace you have been saved, through faith—and this is not from yourselves, it is the gift of God, not by works, so that no one can boast."* - Ephesians 2:8-9

+ Jesus showed us God's amazing grace when He died on the cross.

+ He paid the debt of our sins that we couldn't pay.

+ He gives us forgiveness and freedom while taking our guilt and death on Himself.

+ "Entering into a relationship with God is a gift. Like any gift, we simply receive it with gratitude." - *Jason*

+ "When we become a Christian, the Holy Spirit comes into our lives. He gives us a deep experience of God's love and an unwavering certainty that we're God's very own kids!" - *Ben*

What Does It Mean To Have Faith?

+ Ephesians 2:8 explains that we are saved by grace and through faith.

+ Blondin's mother was the only person willing to put her life in his hands. This demonstrates authentic faith.

+ "Faith is putting our lives in Jesus' hands." - *Jason*

Question Three
If the water in the picture of the swimming pool represents a relationship with God, which person in the picture best represents where you are at?
Refer to image on page 24.

- Would you have described yourself as a different person in the picture at another time in your life?

What Does It Mean To Have Faith? (continued)

+ Faith is leaning our whole weight upon Jesus and what He has done.

+ We can ask God to forgive us for the wrong that we've done. The Bible calls this repentance: it's a change of thinking that leads to a change of living.

+ "As we consider the life, claims and love of Jesus, we have an opportunity to respond in faith." - *Jason*

Discussion Guide

More Questions (choose a few)

- What did you think about today's episode?
- What stood out to you?
- What does the phrase "step of faith" mean to you?
- What other things, besides God, do people put their faith in?
- What do you think it means to have a relationship with God?
- Is there a difference between thinking about Christianity as a religion versus thinking of it as a relationship with God?
- Ben and Jason said that the way to enter into a relationship with God is through faith and repentance, or—in other words—recognizing that we need to turn to God and trust Him. What could hold someone back from taking this step?

> **God never ignores, He never pushes us away, and He never gives us second best.**

Prayer

Jesus gave His life so that we can have a relationship with God. We grow in our relationship with God by communicating with Him through prayer. Prayer is unique for each person. Jesus gave us a model to help us pray (Matthew 6).

Question One

If you could be any superhero, who would you be?

- Or, if you could have any superpower, what would it be and why?
- Did you have a favourite superhero when you were younger?

What Is Prayer?
+ Simply put, prayer is talking to God.

+ 75% of people have admitted to praying at least once a week.

Why Should We Pray?
+ "The truth is: prayer changes things." - *Ben*

+ *"Ask and it will be given to you; seek and you will find; knock and the door will be opened to you. For everyone who asks receives; the one who seeks finds; and to the one who knocks, the door will be opened. Which of you, if your son asks for bread, will give him a stone? Or if he asks for a fish, will give him a snake? If you, then, though you are sinful, know how to give good gifts to your children, how much more will your Father in heaven give good gifts to those who ask him!"* - *Matthew 7:7-11*

+ You can pray about anything—the big things and the seemingly insignificant things.

+ When Jesus gave His life on the cross, He made it possible for us to have a relationship with God.

+ God is not a cosmic vending machine; He is our Heavenly Father.

+ "The story about the boy in the sandbox is less about a rock that needs to be moved and more about a father who wants to be close to his son."
- *Jason*

+ Prayer is all about us growing closer to God.

Question Two

Why do you think people don't always get what they pray for?

- Why would a loving God not always give people what they pray for?
- Have you ever looked back and been thankful that God didn't give you what you prayed for?

....

"For my thoughts are not your thoughts, neither are your ways my ways," declares the Lord. "As the heavens are higher than the earth, so are my ways higher than your ways and my thoughts than your thoughts."
- Isaiah 55:8-9

....

Prayer Brings Peace

+ Jesus calms the storm - Mark 4:35-41

+ *"Do not be anxious about anything, but in every situation, by prayer and petition, with thanksgiving, present your requests to God. And the peace of God, which transcends all understanding, will guard your hearts and your minds in Christ Jesus." - Philippians 4:6-7*

+ "God cares about me, and He cares about my family. I can have peace no matter what's happening." - *Ben*

Question Three

Have you ever tried praying? What did you pray for? What happened?

- In what situation could you imagine yourself praying?
- Did your family pray at all when you were growing up?

....

How Do We Pray?

+ Each one of us needs to find our own regular time and place to talk to God.

+ Prayer is not meant to be a show. It should be simple and from the heart.

Jesus Teaches Us How To Pray (Matthew 6:9-13)

"Our Father in heaven, hallowed be your name."
+ Start your prayers by talking to God with worship and thanks.

"Your kingdom come, your will be done, on earth as it is in heaven."
+ When we pray, we ask for God's plans and purposes to be accomplished in our lives and in the world around us.

"Give us today our daily bread."
+ Ask God for anything you need. He cares about all our needs, big and small.

"And forgive us our debts, as we also have forgiven our debtors."
+ Forgive those who have hurt or offended you, and ask God to forgive you for any wrong you have done.

"And lead us not into temptation but deliver us from the evil one."

+ God wants to give you the strength you need to resist temptation and make right choices.

+ Prayer is the most important part of a relationship with Jesus.

+ Give it a shot! God is listening!

More Questions (choose a few)

- How did you feel about today's episode?
- What stood out to you?
- If God knows all our needs, why should we pray about them?
- If you had to summarize the purpose of prayer, what would you say?
- Ben shared about how he felt after his parents split up and how, after praying, even though the situation didn't change, something in his heart did. Have you ever had a similar experience where you felt God was near in a really hard time?
- When do you think would be a good time and place to pray?

> **We can't miss the main thing: discovering Jesus in its pages.**

Episode SIX | Bible

Bible

The Bible is a book, but it's unlike any other book in the world. It's God's word: His message to all the world. We can trust God to teach us, guide us, and comfort us through the Bible.

The Bible Is Powerful, Precious and Popular

+ It is estimated that more than four billion copies of the Bible have been distributed. That's way more than the *Harry Potter* series, *The Lord of the Rings* trilogy and *The Hunger Games* trilogy combined.

+ The Bible was originally written in Hebrew, Greek and Aramaic, and has been translated into over 2400 languages.

+ The Bible is illegal in many countries, and yet, it is so precious to people that they risk their lives to share it with others.

Question One

What is one of your favourite movies or books?
*Besides the Bible.

- What are your favourite kinds of books or movies?
- Are there any movies or books that you want to read/see?

....

What Is The Bible?

The Bible Is A Book
+ Actually, it's a book filled with more than 60 books.

+ The name Bible comes from the Latin word *biblia* which means "books" or "library of books."

+ It was written over a span of 1500 years by about 40 different authors.

+ It is divided into two main sections: The Old Testament (OT) and The New Testament (NT).

+ The OT was written before Jesus lived on earth and the NT was written after.

The Bible Is More Than A Book

+ *"All Scripture is inspired by God." - 2 Timothy 3:16a*

+ God is the architect of the Bible. He used people to write it, but decided exactly what it would say.

+ "While I was studying at university, I was able to read many of the most influential books ever written, but none of them impacted my life in as profound a way as the Bible." - *Jason*

Question Two

Do you think the Bible has a purpose in the world today? What might it be?

- In one word, how would you describe your initial feeling towards the Bible?
- Do you think there is a difference between the Bible and a self-help book or magazine?
- Why do you think the Bible is read and admired in so many cultures, by so many different people, in so many eras of history?

The Bible In Our Lives

Jesus Is The Main Character
+ "This is amazing: the entire Bible is like one big arrow pointing to Jesus. 'Cause this is the number one thing God wants to show us: Himself." - *Ben*

+ Through the Bible, we see the personality and character of God.

It Guides Us
+ *"Your word is a lamp for my feet, a light on my path." - Psalm 119:105*

+ "The Bible's like a big flashlight guiding us through life. It talks about things we deal with everyday: friends, money, work, sex, pain and joy, just to name a few." - *Jason*

The Bible Leads Us To Relationship With God
+ Reading the Bible is not just about learning facts about God; it invites us to encounter God.

+ "It's so important to read it and study it, but we can't miss the main thing: discovering Jesus in its pages. It's about knowing God through His word." - *Jason*

Question Three

Have you ever tried reading the Bible before? How did it go?

- Have you ever heard somebody teach from the Bible in a way you connected with?
- Do any quotes from the Bible have special meaning for you?

How Do I Read The Bible?
It's helpful to set a regular time and place to read the Bible.

6 Tips For Reading The Bible:
+ Don't flip and point
+ Genre matters
+ Ask lots of questions
+ Pray
+ Talk to people
+ Put it into practice

More Questions (choose a few)

- How did you feel about today's episode?
- What stood out to you?
- Why do you think the Bible is so popular?
- Why would governments not want the Bible in their country?
- What do you think about the idea that the Bible is like a guide for living on earth?
- Has the Bible ever influenced your thoughts or actions?
- Ben and Jason gave 6 tips for reading the Bible (*see list above*). Which one, if any, stood out to you?

> "The way of Jesus is totally unlike the way of this world."

Episode SEVEN | Follow

Follow

God has a great plan for our lives and He guides us into a new and better way of living. As we follow Jesus, our lifestyles are transformed.

....

"We've got to grab onto Jesus and trust Him, because He can see what we can't, and He's guiding us to a full life." - *Ben*

....

Question One

Have you ever been lost before? What happened?

- If you were lost in the wilderness and could choose three things to have with you, what would they be?

....

A New Way Of Living

+ *"Don't copy the behaviour and customs of this world, but let God transform you into a new person by changing the way you think. Then you will learn to know God's will for you."* - Romans 12:2

+ One Bible translator, J.B. Phillips, puts it this way: "Don't let the world around you squeeze you into its mould."[5]

+ "It wasn't really about me being allowed or not allowed to do one thing or another, as if I was afraid God was going to strike me with lightning; but that God really loves me, and has a plan for my life, and He wants what's best for me." - *Jason*

+ God leads us into the fullest life.

Our Relationship With God Impacts The Way We Speak
+ *"With the tongue we praise our Lord and Father, and with it we curse human beings, who have been made in God's likeness. Out of the same mouth come praise and cursing. My brothers and sisters, this should not be." - James 3:9-10*

Following Jesus Transforms The Way We Treat Others
+ As we experience God's love for us, we begin to love others more.

How Does God Guide Us?

+ This episode mentions four different ways that God can guide us through life:
  - The Bible
  - Our Conscience
  - The voice of the Holy Spirit
  - Advice from Others (This comes up between question 2 and 3 in the episode)

Question Two

Are God's instructions old-fashioned and irrelevant or do they still matter today?

- How could the Bible, written so long ago, still be helpful today?
- Do you think God's instructions bring freedom or inhibit freedom?

....

A New Way Of Living (continued)

Our Relationship With God Changes The Way We See Money And Possessions
+ *"I was really impacted by the words of Jesus: 'It's better to give than to receive'" - Kris*

Following Jesus Impacts Our Views On Sexuality

+ "Sex has the power to bring people together, build families and give life. And because it's powerful, it can also cause a lot of damage when it's misused." - *Jason*

New Beginnings

+ "Your yesterday doesn't determine your tomorrow." - *Ben*

+ *"Because of the Lord's great love we are not consumed, for his compassions never fail. They are new every morning; great is your faithfulness." - Lamentations 3:22-23*

+ When a person becomes a Christian, they're a new person. Their identity, the very core of who they are, is changed by Jesus.

+ "God's got a great plan for your life, and He wants to guide you along the way." - *Jason*

Question Three

How do you feel about the idea that God has a plan for your life?

- Do you think God controls our destiny and guides us, or do we control our own destinies?

....

God Is A Good Father Who Wants The Best For Us

+ "God gives us boundaries so that we can enjoy life to the fullest. And this is the great paradox: God's instructions don't restrict us; they make us free." - *Jason*

+ As we pursue God's will in our lives, we can count on Him to lead.

+ *"The Lord is my shepherd, I lack nothing. He makes me lie down in green pastures, he leads me beside quiet waters, he refreshes my soul. He guides me along the right paths for his name's sake. Even though I walk through the darkest valley, I will fear no evil, for you are with me; your rod and your staff, they comfort me."* - Psalm 23:1-4

More Questions (choose a few)

- How did you feel about today's episode?
- What stood out to you?
- What would you tell a friend who told you they'd made a mess of their life?
- Do you find it hard to trust God with your future?
- How has your relationship with God impacted your actions, or the way you talk, or your thoughts?
- Jason said that "The way of Jesus is totally unlike the way of this world." What do you think he means by that?
- Jason and Ben talked about a few different ways that God can speak to us. Have you ever sensed God guiding you through any of the following: the Bible, your conscience, the advice of others, or the Holy Spirit?

> I will give you a new heart and put a new spirit in you.

Ezekiel 36:26

Episode EIGHT | Spirit

Spirit

The Holy Spirit is God at work on earth. Jesus said it would be better for us to have the Holy Spirit. The Holy Spirit is poured out on all people, filling the hearts of God's children with His love and confirming their identity as part of His family.

"God is the best at giving gifts. He knows our deepest heart's desires, and He knows exactly what to give us. We're going to devote the next two sessions to talk about the gift that God gives His people: the Holy Spirit." - *Ben*

Question One

If you were given a million dollars that you had to give away, what would you do with it?

- If you were given a million dollars that you got to keep, what would you do with it?

Who Is The Holy Spirit?

+ The Holy Spirit is God at work on Earth.

+ The Bible describes Him in many ways:

Comforter *Advocate* *Spirit of Wisdom*
Guide *Teacher* *Gift of God*
Spirit of Jesus *Helper*

+ "The Holy Spirit has been working on earth since the day of creation. He's God present at the beginning, and God present with us now." - *Jason*

+ "There is one God who exists eternally as Father, Son and Holy Spirit. One divine Essence, three distinct Persons. The teaching of the Trinity is a mystery that goes beyond reason without opposing it."[6] - *Chris Price*

+ Can you imagine how awesome it would be to have Jesus by your side? And yet, Jesus told His disciples, *"It is best for you that I go away because if I don't, the Holy Spirit won't come, but if I do go away, then I'll send him to you." - John 16:7 (paraphrased)*

The Day Of Pentecost

+ Acts 2 describes the Holy Spirit coming in power on the Day of Pentecost (a festival in Israel).

+ *"In the last days, God says, I will pour out my Spirit on all people. Your sons and daughters will prophesy, your young men will see visions, and your old men will dream dreams. Even on my servants, both men and women, I will pour out my Spirit in those days, and they will prophesy." - Acts 2:17-18*

+ "When the Holy Spirit fell on Pentecost, this changed everything; God was fulfilling His promise to pour out His Spirit on all people who believed."
- *Jason*

Question Two

What questions come to mind when you hear about the Holy Spirit?

- What do you think about the idea that the Holy Spirit is not a force, but a distinct being (in other words, has a personality)?
- The Bible uses many names when referring to the Holy Spirit (*refer to the list on page 41*). Do any of them stand out to you?

....

What Does The Holy Spirit Do?

He Fills Our Hearts With God's Love
+ "God doesn't want us to be unsure of His love for us from one day to the next." - *Jason*

He Assures Us That We Are Part Of God's Family
+ *"The Spirit you received does not make you slaves, so that you live in fear again; rather, the Spirit you received brought about your adoption to sonship. And by him we cry, 'Abba, Father.' The Spirit himself testifies with our spirit that we are God's children." - Romans 8:15-16*

He Makes Us More Like Jesus
+ *"The Holy Spirit produces this kind of fruit in our lives: love, joy, peace, patience, kindness, goodness, faithfulness, gentleness and self-control." - Galatians 5:22-23*

He Gives Us The Power To Overcome Sin And Addiction
+ Christians don't have to find the power inside themselves to overcome destructive habits.

He Empowers Us With Spiritual Gifts

+ "A spiritual gift is given to each of us so we can help each other. *To one person the Spirit gives the **ability to give wise advice;** to another the same Spirit gives a **message of special knowledge**. The same Spirit gives **great faith** to another, and to someone else the Spirit gives the **gift of healing**. He gives one person the **power to perform miracles**, and another the **ability to prophesy**. He gives someone else the **ability to discern whether a message is from the Spirit of God or from another spirit**. Still another person is given the **ability to speak in unknown languages**, while another is given the **ability to interpret what is being said**. It is the one and only Spirit who distributes all these gifts. He alone decides which gift each person should have.*" - 1 Corinthians 12:7-11 (emphasis added)

Question Three

Have you ever heard of, or had any experience with God's supernatural gifts?

*Take extra time on this question to help guests feel more comfortable before the prayer ministry in the next session.

- Have you ever had someone pray with you? How did it go?
- Have you ever felt like God was speaking to you?
- Have you ever had a strong feeling or sense of the love and presence of God?
- Have you, or someone you know personally, ever experienced a miracle?

The Holy Spirit Is For Everyone

+ *"He redeemed us, so that by faith we might receive the promise of the Spirit." - Galatians 3:14 (paraphrased)*

+ *"The promise is for you and your children and for all who are far off—for all whom the Lord our God will call." - Acts 2:39*

+ *"I will give you a new heart and put a new spirit in you; I will remove from you your heart of stone and give you a heart of flesh. And I will put my Spirit in you and move you to follow my decrees and be careful to keep my laws." - Ezekiel 36:26-27*

More Questions (choose a few)

- What did you think about today's episode?
- What stood out to you?
- Have you ever seen someone's life change so much that you couldn't deny it was God changing them?
- Is there any way we can tell if someone else's experience with the Holy Spirit is genuine or not?
- What are some reasons a person might be hesitant to be filled with the Holy Spirit?
- What are some good reasons a person would want to be filled with the Holy Spirit?

> The crippling fear of what others might think or say is replaced with confidence and love.

Fill

God wants all of us to experience being filled with His Holy Spirit. When the Holy Spirit fills our lives, our experience is marked by a profound sense of God's love and power, a boldness to witness, and a renewed desire to praise God. This experience is unique for everyone.

*There are no discussion questions in this episode. The episode is meant to serve as preparation for a time of prayer. For many, this prayer time is the most impactful part of the Alpha experience. To prepare for this session, be sure to watch the Training Session on Prayer Ministry. Plan to set aside 15-45 minutes for prayer and worship following the episode. The goal is to give everyone the opportunity to receive prayer.

Be Filled With The Spirit

+ Like a pilot light in a fireplace or furnace, the Holy Spirit lives within the heart of every Christian.

+ Like turning on the gas, when we're filled with the Holy Spirit, His power, presence and love are released into every part of our lives.

+ "Christians can't ever lose the Spirit, but His filling is something we should constantly pursue."[7] - *Francis Chan*

+ Acts 8 describes Philip spreading the good news about Jesus in Samaria, resulting in many new believers. Peter and John arrived later and prayed for these new Christians to receive the Holy Spirit.

+ *"Do not get drunk on wine, which leads to debauchery. Instead, be filled with the Spirit." - Ephesians 5:18*

Go On Being Filled
+ We need to continually be filled with the Spirit just as we must continually be loving towards others.

\+ "The crux of it, I believe, is being filled with the Spirit is not a one-time act. Being filled with the Spirit is not limited to the day we first met Christ. Instead, throughout Scripture we read of a relationship that calls us into an active pursuit of the Spirit."[8] - *Francis Chan*

\+ "Sometimes people get tripped up wondering, 'Am I filled with the Holy Spirit or not?' or they look around and wonder, 'Is that person filled with the Holy Spirit?' But this way of thinking misses the point entirely: when I hear about all the Holy Spirit does, I get a deep desire in my heart for more of God. I want all that God has for me." - *Jason*

What Happens When We're Filled With The Holy Spirit?

Power

\+ When the Holy Spirit showed up in power on the day of Pentecost, and in every other time in the Book of Acts, there was a noticeable response in the life of each person.

\+ Each person's response to the Holy Spirit is unique.

\+ As you pray, don't chase an experience of God's power. Instead, chase God Himself.

\+ The Holy Spirit can help us with words that our minds may not even understand.

\+ In Acts 2 and again in Acts 10, believers praised God in different languages or "tongues". The most common place for speaking in tongues is during personal prayer.

Praise

\+ Praise is the most natural response to the work of the Spirit in our lives. As you pray, you might have a deep desire to worship and give thanks to God.

\+ "For many people, when God's Spirit touches their hearts they experience an emotional response: tears of relief or joy, a new feeling of passion for life, laughter, happiness, or a deep sense of being loved." - *Jason*

+ *"May the God of hope fill you with all joy and peace as you trust in him, so that you may overflow with hope by the power of the Holy Spirit."*
- Romans 15:13

Boldness

+ When we're filled with the Holy Spirit, we experience increased courage and passion to tell others about God.

+ Acts 4 says that the disciples prayed and were filled with the Holy Spirit, and as a result they went out and spoke about God boldly.

+ "We have the firm certainty that the Holy Spirit gives the Church with His mighty breath, the courage to persevere, to bring the gospel to the ends of the earth."[9] - *Pope Francis (paraphrased)*

Love

+ *"God's love has been poured into our hearts through the Holy Spirit, who has been given to us." - Romans 5:5*

Will Anything Hold Us Back?

+ Luke 11:9-13 describes praying for the Holy Spirit and what sorts of obstacles we might face.

Doubt

+ *"If you sinful people know how to give good gifts to your children, how much more will your heavenly Father give the Holy Spirit to those who ask him." - Luke 11:13*

Fear

+ *"You fathers—if your children ask for a fish, do you give them a snake instead? Or if they ask for an egg, do you give them a scorpion? Of course not!" - Luke 11:11-12*

Feeling Unworthy

+ God loves us and wants to give us good gifts, not because we deserve them or earned them. He gives us good things because of who He is— our loving heavenly Father.

Thoughts On Prayer Response

+ The purpose of this time of prayer response is to give everyone an opportunity to open their hearts to the work of the Holy Spirit.

+ As you pray, don't rush. Take time to wait.

+ Every prayer time will look different. There is no perfect recipe.

+ One of the leaders can explain the prayer time to all of the guests, pray for the whole group, and give guests an opportunity to pray on their own.

+ This can be followed by small group hosts and helpers asking each guest individually if they would like to receive prayer. Don't force anyone to pray.

+ This could be followed by a time of worship and response to the unique things God is doing in your group.

+ Training Episode 3 on Prayer Ministry goes into more detail about how to prepare for and facilitate this time of prayer.

> **We stand in the doorway between two kingdoms.**

Episode TEN | Evil

Evil

The Devil is the source of much of the evil that we experience in our lives and see in the world around us. He hates God and God's people and his mission is to spite God by hurting what God loves most—human beings. The Devil tempts us, lies to us and accuses us, but God has given us all we need to take a stand against the Devil's work in our lives.

Question One

Who is your favourite super villain?

- Who do you think is the scariest?
- If you were a super villain, what would be your name?

....

The Devil

+ "For some people, believing in the Devil is easier than believing in God, becausethey can see so much radical evil all around us." - *Jason*

+ Much of the evil in the world comes from selfish, hurtful choices made by people, but the Bible tells us that there are also evil spiritual forces at work in the world.

+ In Isaiah 14, there are hints that the Devil is a fallen angel who rebelled against God.

+ In the New Testament, the Devil—also known as Satan or the Enemy— is described as a personal, spiritual being who hates God and has leadership over many demons like himself.

+ *"Take your stand against the devil's schemes. For our struggle is not against flesh and blood, but against the rulers, against the authorities, against the powers of this dark world and against the spiritual forces of evil in the heavenly realms."* - Ephesians 6:11-12

+ *"The thief comes only to steal and kill and destroy; I have come that they may have life, and have it to the full." - John 10:10*

+ The Devil wants to destroy everything God has made. He hates it. We don't have to be afraid, though, because the Enemy only has a few techniques: he lies, he tempts, and he accuses.

What Does The Devil Do?

He Tempts
+ "This much is sure, every time the Devil tries to tempt you, he does it with the intent to hurt you." - *Jason*

+ Sin takes you further than you want to go, keeps you longer than you want to stay, and costs you more than you want to pay.

He Accuses
+ In Revelation 12:10b, it says that the Devil accuses God's people day and night.

+ There is a difference between God's voice of conviction and the Enemy's voice of condemnation. God's conviction is clear and specific: it points to something in our lives that He wants us to change, while condemnation feels like a blanket of shame, guilt and hopelessness.

+ The Devil wants to weigh you down with guilt and shame. Jesus wants to set you free.

He Lies
+ "In John 8, Jesus calls the Devil 'the father of lies', as if to say, he lies about everything. He lies to us about God, about what is right and wrong, and about ourselves." - *Ben*

+ The enemy wants us to believe the lie that God's love and promises are for other people, but not for us.

Discussion Guide

Question Two

What are some common lies that people believe about themselves? Or about God?

- What kind of lies do girls tell themselves? How about guys?
- Where do we get these lies from?

....

The Power Of Jesus

+ *"For [God] has rescued us from the dominion of darkness and brought us into the kingdom of the Son he loves." - Colossians 1:13*

+ *"Jesus pulls us out of the enemy's grip and firmly plants us in the safety of God's family." - Jason*

+ Through the cross, Jesus disarmed the evil powers and authorities. In Jesus, we have that same power and authority over the Enemy.

How Can We Stand Against The Enemy?
+ Remember truth found in the Bible
+ Be strengthened in prayer
+ Hold firm in faith
+ Allow the Holy Spirit to lead and strengthen

The Now-And-Not-Yet Kingdom Of God

+ Jesus announced that the kingdom of God had come, and yet He also taught that it was something coming in the future.

+ We stand in the doorway between two kingdoms, like the eleven months between D-Day and VE Day of World War Two.

+ "[The enemy's] going down swinging and trying to take down everyone he can on his way out. But God's unending kingdom is infinitely more powerful."
- *Jason*

Question Three

What can people do to fight against evil in their lives and in the world?

- Can you think of an example of one person making a big difference?
- We can use our time, our talents, our money, and our influence to resist evil in the world. Take a few minutes to talk about the ways that we can do good, even with the limitations we have.

....

Overcome Evil With Good

+ It wouldn't be wise for us to ignore the Devil or pretend he doesn't exist, or to become obsessed with him.

+ There are clear warnings in the Bible against witchcraft and other occult practices because they open us up to darkness.

+ Jesus taught His disciples to pray: *"Your kingdom come, your will be done, on earth as it is in heaven."* - *Matthew 6:10*

+ "Jesus demonstrated a life that pushed back the darkness in the world."
- *Ben*

+ "[Some] believe it is only great power that can hold evil in check. That is not what I found: I found it is the small, everyday deeds of ordinary folk that keep the darkness at bay—small acts of kindness and love."[10]
- *Gandalf, The Hobbit: An Unexpected Journey*

"Do not be overcome by evil, but overcome evil with good."
- Romans 12:21

More Questions (choose a few)

- What did you think about today's episode?
- What stood out to you?
- What is an example of evil at work in the world today?
- Ben and Jason said that the Devil has three tactics: he lies to us, accuses us, and tempts us. Can you think of a time in your life when you've experienced one of these?
- Jason and Ben mentioned that there is often a spiritual struggle as we get closer to God. Have you experienced this, in any way, on your spiritual journey?

> **We can experience the reality of God's kingdom. It's marked by peace and joy and love and healing.**

Episode ELEVEN | Healing

Discussion Guide

Healing

In heaven there will be no more suffering or pain, but while we are here on earth we are invited to pray for glimpses of heaven to collide with earth. God is a healer. It's part of His character. Everyone is invited to ask God for physical healing. While not everyone will be healed instantly, we can expect to experience moments of God's healing power demonstrated as we pray.

For Question 3 of this episode we decided not to include street interviews. Encourage your group to share stories of pain and healing.

There are no additional questions at the end of this session. You can use the time to facilitate prayer for people to receive healing. To prepare for this session, watch Training Episode 3 on "Prayer Ministry" for guidelines to facilitate the prayer time.

Question One

What is your most embarrassing moment?

- Would you rather give an unprepared speech in front of your class or sing a solo without any musical accompaniment?

....

God The Healer

+ "All I could think was, 'Jesus is about to heal me!' And I have never been that confident of something in my entire life." - *Krystle*

+ *"I am the Lord, your healer."* - *Exodus 15:26*

+ All through the Gospels we read about Jesus repeatedly healing people.

+ Healing is in God's character, and it's part of His love for us.

+ God's power and willingness to heal is demonstrated in the Old Testament, in the life of Jesus, in the early Church, and in the world today.

Question Two

Do you believe that God heals people today? Why or why not?

- What do you think about Krystle's story?
- Physical healing isn't the only type of healing someone can experience. What are some other ways someone could be healed?

...

The Kingdom Of God

+ "The kingdom of God isn't a geographical space. It captures the idea of God's rule and reign in any city or country around the world." - *Ben*

+ 2,000 years ago, Jesus sent the Holy Spirit and this marked a new era of God's kingdom.

+ *"Jesus went through all the towns and villages, teaching in their synagogues, proclaiming the good news of the kingdom and healing every disease and sickness."* - *Matthew 9:35*

+ God's kingdom is marked by peace, joy, love and healing. Broken things are made new, lost things are found, and tears are wiped away.

+ Jesus told his disciples that He would return one day. This would mark the beginning of a new era. There are over 300 references in the New Testament to the second coming of Jesus.

+ The kingdom of God is here and now, and yet, we anticipate a day in the future, when Christ will return and the fullness of God's kingdom will be revealed.

Healing Today

+ "In Matthew 10, Jesus gives His disciples authority to heal the sick. And it wasn't just limited to them. In Luke 10, He's with 72 of His followers, and He sends them out to do the exact same thing. And then it gets more exciting: the Word of God invites us—that's me and you—to participate in healing."
- *Jason*

+ 1 Corinthians 12 describes spiritual gifts that God gives to His children, including gifts of healing.

+ Nowhere in the Bible does it mention that these gifts are limited to a certain period of time or to a small group of people. All of God's children are invited to ask for and receive healing.

+ "We're free and able to ask the Holy Spirit at any time to heal us. But if the Spirit does not do it, there is no reason to think that it is because we have no faith or because God does not love us or is punishing us."[11] - *Father Raniero Cantalamessa (The Preacher to the Papal Household)*

+ "Some of us can relate to the miracles we've shared, and others of us know the feeling of loss too." - *Jason*

+ When people experience healing, their faith increases. Even when there is no healing, people often feel closer to God as they sense His presence and peace.

+ Regardless of the results of our prayers for healing, God wants to meet each of us in the middle of what we are going through.

Question Three

Take a few minutes to talk about any experiences you may have had with sickness and healing.

- Have you ever prayed for someone to be healed? What happened?
- How do we make sense of the times God doesn't heal someone when we ask?
- Have you ever been sick or injured and had someone pray for you to be healed?
- Have you heard of anyone being healed supernaturally?
- What do you think of ordinary people praying for others to be healed?

Praying For Healing

+ Each one of us is invited to be prayed for and to pray for others.

+ God does the healing, not us. There are no magic techniques or secrets.

+ When we pray for God to heal, we can:
  - Pray in Jesus' name
  - Lay hands on people when appropriate
  - Ask God for wisdom and discernment
  - Ask the person being prayed for how he or she is feeling

+ One pastor used to say, "When we pray for no one, no one gets healed. Instead, we pray for everyone and not everyone's healed, but some are."

+ "I wonder if you'll give this a try: would you let someone pray for a need that you may have? Or maybe you'll be brave enough and have the faith to pray for someone who needs healing!" - *Ben*

+ The kingdom of God is here and now, and yet, we anticipate a day in the future, when Christ will return and the fullness of God's kingdom will be revealed.

> **Following Jesus is life's great adventure!**

Church

The Christian Church is God's family. Jesus started with 12 disciples and today there are more than 2 billion Christians in the world because people have passed on the message of Jesus to others. The Bible encourages everyone to be part of a local community of Christians and to share the message of Jesus with others.

Question One

What is your favourite viral video?

- If you could go back in time and capture any moment on camera, what moment would you film?
- If you had to create a video to get millions of views online, what would you do?

....

Christianity Is Not A Solo Sport

+ "Christianity is not, and was never intended to be, a one-man journey or a solo sport. If you flip open your Bible and read the book of Acts, you quickly discover that the very first Christians ate together, served the poor together, prayed together, worshipped together, and studied the Bible together. The picture we get of the early Church is of a growing community of people celebrating together the new life that they've found in Jesus." - *Ben*

+ Jesus started with 12 disciples. Today there are more than 2,000,000,000 Christians on the planet.

\+ The early Christians had a deep conviction and passion to tell others about Jesus. The good news began to spread from one person to another.

\+ "Imagine being stranded on a desert island with a small group of people. If you found water, of course the loving thing to do would be to tell the rest of the group. And in the same way, we know so many people who are overwhelmed with guilt and scared of death and burdened by sin. And the gospel, the good news of Jesus, is like fresh water. To keep Jesus a secret is like hiding water from thirsty people." - *Jason*

\+ *"Go and make disciples of all nations." - Matthew 28:19 (paraphrased)*

\+ Joey's story reminds us that living a Christian life helps to draw people to God.

Question Two

Is it okay to tell others about Jesus? What stops people from doing it?

- What do you think is a respectful way to talk to others about Jesus?
- Have you ever had a negative experience with this? Or have you ever had a positive experience with this?

What Is The Church?

The People Of God

\+ The Church is not limited to a building. The Church around the world is the family of God.

\+ "In Ephesians (2:19-22), it says that the church is a building built out of people, and Jesus is the chief cornerstone—the part that holds it all together." - *Ben*

+ Even though there are some things that Christians may disagree on, the things that unite us are much bigger and are far more important.

+ John 17 records Jesus praying that as Christians we would be united as one.

+ For centuries, Christians have been persecuted and even martyred, but the Church continues to grow.

The Body Of Christ

+ Just like our physical body has different parts that work together, the Church has many parts and each person plays a unique and important part. Every part matters.

+ "God uses the Church to be His hands and feet around the world." - *Ben*

+ Throughout history, the Church has led the way in responding to needs around the world.

Question Three

Do you see any difference in being part of a church?

- Do you notice any difference in people you know who go to church?
- Can attending church be a negative thing? How?

....

Being Part Of The Church

+ "We're made for community. Gathering as the Church is a necessary step to keep your relationship with God alive." - *Jason*

+ "It's a privilege to gather together with other Christians. Come and be a part of the Church and a youth group. And don't just show up—commit! Get involved. Be the Church." - *Ben*

+ "Pray for your friends. Pray that they would meet Jesus. Ask God to give you the words to say at just the right time, and the ability to listen in a whole new way. Live your life as an example of someone who's loved by God and is learning to love others more." - *Jason*

This is just the beginning. The journey has just begun.

Following Jesus is life's great adventure!

More Questions (choose a few)

- What did you think about today's episode?
- What stood out to you?
- Why do you think that the Church has managed to grow in spite of so much persecution and opposition?
- What do you think about the idea that "church is people, not a building"?
- What would you say to someone who is afraid of others knowing they are a Christian?
- Has your time at Alpha impacted your perspective on faith, life, and Jesus? If yes, how?
- Is there anyone in your life you think would enjoy an opportunity to be part of Alpha?

*During this final small group time, distribute a copy of the Guest Feedback Form to each person and allow time to complete it. Use the responses to help you improve the Alpha experience for future guests.

END NOTES

1. "Rock On Freddie." Interview by Freddie Mercury. Queen Archives. N.p., n.d. Web. 02 May 2014. <http://www.queenarchives.com/index.php?title=Freddie_Mercury_-_XX-XX-1985_-_Unknown>.
2. Lewis, C. S. *God in the Dock: Essays on Theology and Ethics.* Grand Rapids: Eerdmans, 1970. Print.
3. 7-Week Alpha Course Promo. Perf. Jamie Haith. AlphaCanada, 2012. YouTube Video.
4. 7-Week Alpha Course Promo. Perf. Jamie Haith. AlphaCanada, 2012. YouTube Video.
5. The New Testament in Modern English. New York: Macmillan, 1958. Print.
6. Price, Chris. *Suffering With God: A Thoughtful Reflection on Evil, Suffering and Finding Hope beyond Band-aid Solutions.* N.p.: CreateSpace Independent Platform, 2014. Print.
7. Chan, Francis, and Danae Yankoski. *Forgotten God: Reversing Our Tragic Neglect of the Holy Spirit.* Colorado Springs, CO: David C. Cook, 2009. Print.
8. Chan, Francis, and Danae Yankoski. *Forgotten God: Reversing Our Tragic Neglect of the Holy Spirit.* Colorado Springs, CO: David C. Cook, 2009. Print.
9. De Souza, Raymond J., Father. "Look at St. Francis to Understand Pope Francis." National Post. Postmedia Network Inc., 15 Mar. 2013. Web. 3 May 2014.
10. The Hobbit: An Unexpected Journey. Dir. Peter Jackson. Perf. Martin Freeman, Ian McKellen, Richard Armitage. New Line Cinema, 2012. Film.
11. Alpha USA. "Does God Heal Today?" Alpha USA Website. Alpha USA, 2014. Web. 03 May 2014.

Alpha USA
1635 Emerson Lane
Naperville, IL 60540

800.362.5742
212.406.5269

info@alphausa.org
alphausa.org
alpharesources.org

@alphausa

Alpha in the Caribbean
Holy Trinity Brompton
Brompton Road
London SW7 1JA UK

+44 (0) 845.644.7544

americas@alpha.org
caribbean.Alpha.org

@AlphaCaribbean

Alpha Canada
Suite #230
11331 Coppersmith Way
Richmond, BC V7A 5J9

800.743.0899

office@alphacanada.org
alphacanada.org

Purchase resources in Canada:

Parasource
Canada
P.O. Box 98, 55 Woodslee Avenue
Paris, ON N3L 3E5

800.263.2664

custserv@parasource.com
parasource.com

CPSIA information can be obtained
at www.ICGtesting.com
Printed in the USA
LVHW06s2051280318
571379LV00006B/56/P